Sixty Miles to Silver Lake

by Dan LeFranc

A SAMUEL FRENCH ACTING EDITION

SAMUEL FRENCH

FOUNDED 1830

NEW YORK HOLLYWOOD LONDON TORONTO

SAMUELFRENCH.COM

ISBN 978-0-573-69667-1   Printed in U.S.A.   #29076

IMPORTANT BILLING AND CREDIT
REQUIREMENTS

All producers of *SIXTY MILES TO SILVER LAKE must* give credit to the Author of the Play in all programs distributed in connection with performances of the Play, and in all instances in which the title of the Play appears for the purposes of advertising, publicizing or otherwise exploiting the Play and/or a production. The name of the Author *must* appear on a separate line on which no other name appears, immediately following the title and *must* appear in size of type not less than fifty percent of the size of the title type.

In addition the following credit *must* be given in all programs and publicity information distributed in association with this piece:

World Premiere produced by Page 73 Productions
In association with Soho Repertory Theatre, Inc.

The world premiere of *SIXTY MILES TO SILVER LAKE* opened at Soho Rep, in New York City on January 15, 2009. The production was directed by Anne Kauffman with the following cast and creative team:

KY . . . . Joseph Adams
DENNY . . . . Dane DeHaan

Voiceover – Michael D'Addario
Set and Costume Design – Dane Laffrey
Lighting Design – Tyler Micoleau
Projection/Sound Designer – Leah Gelpe
Production Manager – James E. Cleveland
Company Mananger – Gretchen Margaroli
Production Stage Manager – Rebecca Goldstein-Glaze

Assistant Director – Alice Reagan
Assistant Set and Costume Designer – Hallie Stern
Assistant Lighting Designer – Lee Terry
Assistant Projection/Sound Designer – Nick Gorczynski
Assistant Company Manager – Faiz Osman
Technical Director – Steve Lorick, Jr.
Master Electrician – Jared Welch
Props Master – Mary Robinette Kowal
Deck Automation – Bruno Fontaine
Projection/Sound Operator – Kimberly Ann Fuhr
Run Crew – Eric Web

CHARACTERS

KY
DENNY
The Car

THOUGHT:
The pauses should feel itchy
Like
when you're riding in a car
on a hot, hot day
for so, so long
and you're sweating so much
that your back's
glued to the pleather
of your dad's used car

Without the dedication and support of the following people (and many, many others), this play would not have been possible:

Anne Kauffman, Asher Richelli & Liz Jones, Sarah Benson, Rob Mercato, Dane DeHaan, Joseph Adams, Paula Vogel, Bonnie Metzgar, Naomi Iizuka, Val Day, Erin Cressida Wilson, Cory Hinkle, Scott Raker, Paul Wann, Makaela Pollock, Reed Birney, Jedadiah Schultz, Tim Hopper, Emily Shooltz, Sarah Stern, Mia Rovegno, and the entire LeFranc family.

For The 5

A Moving Car:

A Father and Son seat-belted inside

A fast food Bag crumpled on the floor
A fast food Cup rattling softly in the cup holder

The Son's face is pressed against the rolled-up window

His name's Denny. Denny's dressed for Weekend Soccer
Hair stuck to his face from dried afternoon sweat
Long socks rolled down to his cleats
Shin guards exposed
His Cobalt-Colored Uniform dirt-strewn and grass-stained

Denny's a Down and Dirty Kid

The Father drives

His name's Ky
Ky's dressed like a man who Works Weekends
His tie loosened
The top button of his shirt undone
His Coat outstretched in the backseat

Ky's a Down and Dirty Divorced

A Long Moment of Silence
underscored by the Low Hum of a Car in Motion

Denny gets squirrelly
He blows against the glass
The glass Fogs
He lazily doodles in the fog with his finger
till the fog and doodle vanish

DENNY. Is there anything fun to do in Silver Lake?

Ky checks the rearview

Pause

DENNY. Dad –

> *No Response*

> *Denny props an elbow against the car door*

> man
> This Sucks

> *Pause*

> *Denny blows against the window
> and doodles till it vanishes*

DENNY. this guy on my team
> Matt Arnold
> he was talking to Chris Ying after practice on Wednesday
> Coach Ying's Chris Ying's Dad so Chris knows Everything
> and Chris Ying told Matt Arnold that Coach Ying might nominate me for Spring All-Stars

KY. That's great, Squirt

> *Denny picks at the window*

DENNY. you know
> the coaches they pick for Spring All-Stars almost Always coach for Club

KY. Sounds like fun

> *Denny picks at the window*

DENNY. Sooo
> if I make Spring All-Stars then I have a really good shot at making Club next Fall

> *Ky scans the road*

KY. Which way do I turn on La Paz?

> *Denny rolls his eyes*

> *He Mumbles*

DENNY. right

KY. What?

DENNY. I just said –

KY. You were mumbling –

DENNY. No I wasn't –

KY. well I can't find the Freeway if you can't Enunciate –

DENNY. I said Right

> *Ky gets in the Right Turn Lane*

KY. Okay

> Thank you

> *Pause*

KY. How much is that gonna Cost?

DENNY. what?

KY. the Soccer thing

DENNY. Club

KY. Right

> Club

DENNY. Depends on the team

KY. well

> Your mother get off her ass and find a job yet?

> *Denny picks at the window*

DENNY. She's weighing her options

KY. her Options?

DENNY. yeah

KY. Would you say she spends more time Weighing Potential Employment Opportunities
> or Buying Crap off the Internet?

DENNY. How would I know?

KY. Hazard a Guess

DENNY. I don't know

KY. okay

> well Maybe you should Remind your mother that we still share a Mastercard Account

> and unless eBay's started auctioning off Jobs recently –

DENNY. she's holding out for the Right One

KY. The Right One?

DENNY. yeah

> She's not just gonna take any Stupid Job cuz the Capitalist Machine tells her she's not a Complete Human Being without one

Small Pause

Ky rolls his eyes

KY. okay

> So until the Right One Magically Falls into her Lap
> who's gonna pay for this Club thing?

DENNY. I don't know

KY. well Try to see the Big Picture, Denny
> cuz I don't know how much it costs to play on one of those Teams
> but my Guess is it's not Cheap
> and if your mother refuses to work –

DENNY. Can't you pay for it?
> I mean
> You could afford it, right?

KY. The point is Not whether I can afford it or not

DENNY. Then what's the point?

KY. The point is –
> Your mother has a responsibility to you

DENNY. You have a responsibility to me too

KY. that's right
> a Responsibility that I fulfill –

DENNY. Then how come you haven't paid Child Support in three months?

KY. That's not True –

DENNY. Mom says you're gonna go to Jail if you don't start paying –

KY. Look
> Your Mother needs to stop spending all her time Inventing Lies about me
> and start Waiting Tables

DENNY. She hates Waiting Tables

KY. Well she's good at it
She's an Excellent Waitress
in fact
It's the Only thing I've seen her do with any Success

They hit the Freeway

Ky cranes his neck back and forth

KY. Can you believe this Guy?

Ky cranes his neck back and forth

KY. Come on Buddy
You wanna let me Merge?

Ky cranes his neck

KY. Okay
Okay
Jesus
Thank You!

Ky raises his hand Ironically
Ky shakes his head
He mutters to himself

KY. prick

The Car cruises along at open freeway speed

Ky sighs
Denny watches the landscape zoom by

Pause

Ky chuckles to himself
Denny looks confused

DENNY. what?

KY. you know
Your Mom was Waitressing when we Met
At El Torito

DENNY. okay

KY. I was there for lunch and she uh
     she spilled this Huge Caesar Salad on me
     and it's a Mess
     I mean A Mess
     so she's apologizing and I'm trying to tell her it's Okay
     it's Okay
     but then she starts to brush the dressing off my Pants
     and your Dad's like "Wooo! Hello! Now that's what I
     call Service!"

     Ky laughs
     he tousles Denny's hair

DENNY. you've told this story

KY. Not the Whole Thing

DENNY. Dad

     Ky acquiesces
     He turns on the A/C

     Denny shivers

     He curls up against the window
     He blows
     He doodles till it vanishes

KY. How is your Mom, huh?
     She seeing anybody?

     No Response

KY. I thought I saw her standing next to some Guy
     He one of the Dads from your Team or what?
     You know who I'm talking about?
     Kinda Tall
     Jewish-lookin

     Denny just watches the landscape zoom by

     Pause

     Denny shivers

DENNY. It's like fuckin Siberia in here

KY. Hey
    Language

Denny shivers

DENNY. Seriously
    are you Trying to give me pneumonia?

KY. You know
    more people Die on the 5 than on any other freeway
    in California

DENNY. So?

KY. So the cold keeps me Alert

DENNY. whatever
    you're such a Freak

KY. Oh yeah?
    Tell that to my Insurance Bill
    These Days you make One Mistake and you pay for it
    the Rest of Your Life

Ky checks the Side Mirrors

KY. You know
    you could learn a few things from the way I Drive

DENNY. right

KY. I'm just saying
    now that you're old enough to get your Driver's Permit
    you could afford to pick up some Good Habits

DENNY. I can't get my Driver's Permit for five months

KY. You get it when you turn Fifteen

DENNY. Fifteen and a Half

KY. well it Never Hurts to be Prepared

DENNY. I watch Mom drive all the time

KY. your Mom drives for Shit

DENNY. Whatever
    she drives Fine

KY. She's from Boston, Squirt
    Boston drivers make Californians look like Saints

DENNY. you're from Boston too

KY. no

  I'm from Somerville, Denny

  Somerville's Completely Different

DENNY. yeah well she's still a Way Better Driver than you

  Pause

KY. you know what, Squirt

  It's Absolutely Silly to get yourself wrapped up in all
  this Soccer stuff

  I mean

  this AYDO thing your mom's got you signed up for –

DENNY. AYSO

KY. AYSO

  whatever

DENNY. It's not Whatever

  It's the American Youth Soccer Organization

KY. no

  I'll tell you what it is

  it's Bullshit

  I mean look at the Scam they're pulling, Squirt:

  These assholes Gouge hard-working parents' wallets

  so they can enjoy the "Privilege" of watching their children run after a Ball for a few hours

  And the kids?

  They fill your heads with a bunch of crap about becom-
  ing Professional Soccer Players

  when Everyone Knows

  some Colombian Kid is just gonna sneak across the
  Border with a balloon of Heroin shoved up his ass and
  blow everyone out of the Water

  Seriously

  They should just call this AYDO thing what it is:

  Daycare with Cleats

  Ky shakes his head

KY. You know what the two biggest Scams in America are?
I'll tell you:
Kids Soccer
and the Catholic Church

these Scam Artists make a fortune selling Lies and
False Hope
Not to mention they're both run by a Cabal of Child
Molesters

you know
I was an Altar Boy when I was your age
and the way some of those Priests Looked at Me:
My ass gets Tense just thinking about it

and these Kids' Coaches?

There was an email going around the Office about this
One Guy
Just Disgusting:
When his Boys did Sit-Ups
he'd sit down in the Grass
where he could get a Real Good Look up their Shorts
and Jerk Himself Off right there on the Field in front
of Everyone

Can you Believe that?

They're Wolves
Wolves with Whistles

Seriously Denny
Watch our for that Coach of yours

Long Pause

Denny presses his forehead against the window
He fiddles with his seatbelt strap

DENNY. How come you didn't let Chris come with?

KY. cuz These Weekends are about spending time with
Your Dad
Not your Friends

DENNY. Can Chris come with Next Week?

KY. What did I just say?

DENNY. come on

 He's got the new Tony Hawk

KY. Great

 so you can spend the Entire Weekend in front of a
Television?

DENNY. well How else am I supposed to play it?

KY. Your Mom find a Job yet?

DENNY. What's that have to do with anything?

KY. She's the one who should be buying you that stuff

DENNY. She won't buy it for me cuz she says it sends a Bad
Message to Kids cuz the Skaters in the game don't
wear Helmets

KY. oh That's ridiculous

DENNY. That's what I said

KY. you know She's unbelievable sometimes

 Small Pause

KY. I tell you what

 When we get to Silver Lake

 I'll get you the New Tony Hawk

DENNY. then Can Chris come over next week to play it?

KY. What do you need that kid for if you have the game?

DENNY. cuz he knows all the Hacks

 He like Lives for that stuff

KY. No

DENNY. Come On

 he told me about this One Code where you can skate
as Darth Maul and he's got his Light Saber Bo from
Episode I and whenever you pull off a killer trick he
says "YOU ARE NO MATCH FOR THE SITH, JEDI"

KY. Hey

 keep Pushing Me and you don't get Squat

DENNY. Dad

KY. I'm Serious

Pause

DENNY. Chris Ying's one of my top five Best Friends and everything

but he's probably the Weakest Forward we have

Like

it's so Obvious that the Only Reason he gets to play Four Quarters every game and No One Else ever does is cuz Coach Ying's his Dad

His Dad'll do Anything for him which is so totally not fair I mean

there's like a Word for that, right?

Dad?

Pause
Denny fiddles with his seatbelt strap

DENNY. Can we go to Disneyland?

KY. No

DENNY. Why?

KY. because it's Disneyland

DENNY. Chris told me about this one time Coach Ying took him to Disneyland and they went on the Matterhorn and it's like this Super Fast Ride with a Monster only it's even Cooler cuz the Matterhorn's like a Real Mountain with Real Live Snow

KY. oh come on, Squirt

it's Disneyland

None of it's Real

Pause

Ky checks the rearview
The Low Hum of a Car in Motion

Denny fiddles with the Door Handle a little
He pulls it a few times
but since the door's Locked
it doesn't Open

He keeps fiddling

KY. Denny

DENNY. what?

KY. The last thing I need is for you to go Flying out of the
    Car

DENNY. The door's Locked

KY. I'm not fuckin around
    If the door's faulty –

DENNY. If it's faulty then you can sue Volvo for Tons of
    Money and pay Child Support

Ky pinches Denny
Not too hard
but Enough

DENNY. ow!

    You ever heard of a Joke?

Denny exaggerates the pain

DENNY. ooooow

Ky doesn't buy it

Pause

KY. hey

    How's your Mom, huh?

    She uh
    seeing anyone?

Denny spies the crumpled fast food bag
picks it up
and looks inside

DENNY. Did you get me anything?

KY. I didn't know you wanted something

DENNY. I just played Four Full Quarters

KY. well If you'd communicate these things to me ahead of
    time –

DENNY. well If you ever came to my Games / you'd know
    this stuff –

KY. I have to Work on Saturdays –

DENNY. I'm hungry

KY. well it's Too Late now
We've got Dinner Plans

DENNY. what kind of Dinner Plans?

KY. It's a surprise

DENNY. what kind of Surprise?

KY. well it wouldn't be Much of a Surprise if I told you –

DENNY. there's an In-N-Out at the next Exit

KY. We're running Late as it is
and In-N-Out's just gonna Ruin your appetite

DENNY. All I want are some Fries

KY. Denny
If the Dodgers Game lets out before we make it to LA
the 5's gonna be a Nightmare

DENNY. come on Get Off
I'm Starving

KY. If you really want something
there's a Granola Bar in the glove compartment

DENNY. Granola Bars taste like Ass

KY. well then Tough Shit

Denny stares out the windshield with a Sour Glare
Pause

KY. hey why don't you turn on the Game?
Huh?
come on
they're playing the Angels

DENNY. Baseball's Gay

KY. oh Baseball's Gay
Right
This Coming from the Kid who likes to watch a Bunch
of Immigrants run around in Short Shorts for five
hours

DENNY. It's still way less Gay than Baseball

Pause

DENNY. you know
>Mom lets me get In-N-Out after every single game
>sometimes she even has it waiting for me right when I
>walk off the field
>and she always orders my Double-Double exactly how
>I like it:
>Animal Style No Onions No Tomatoes

KY. Oh yeah?
>well maybe from now on
>I'll buy the In-N-Out
>and your Mom can foot the Bill for that Club Team
>How's that?

>*Denny gets squirrelly*
>*He props a dirty cleat on the dash*

KY. What have I said about shoes on the dash?

>*Denny stares straight ahead*
>*Foot on the dash*

KY. Come on Denny
>your Cleats are Filthy

>*Denny doesn't move*

DENNY. There's no Legroom

KY. Excuse me?

DENNY. Your car's too small
>My legs get cramped

KY. Well when you can Afford your own Car
>you're welcome to Bitch all you want
>but until then Get Your Filthy Cleats off my Dashboard

>*The Dirty Cleat remains*

KY. if you wanna keep testing me
>I've got some Armor-All in the trunk
>I'll make you clean the Hell outta that Dashboard all
>by yourself
>I swear to god

>*The Dirty Cleat remains*

KY. Okay I'm giving you Three Seconds to get your Cleats
off the Dash or
you know What
you'll be Scrubbin this Entire Car Inside/Out All
Weekend

The Dirty Cleat remains

KY. Okay!
I am Counting!

one –
Denny
I mean it
I've got some stuff at home so strong it'll Fry your
Brain Cells
You'll be scrubbin this sucker So Deep
you'll wish you were Gluing Sneakers in Taiwan

two –
I swear to God Denny
if this is how you want to spend our Weekend Together
that's fine by me
Just Keep It Up

Three!
Okay?
I said Three!

Denny scowls
He Very Slowly removes his foot from the dash
Ky drives

KY. hey
guess who I saw the other day?
Pretty Cool

DENNY. who?

KY. that Actor
uh what's his name
you know
from that Movie we saw last weekend

DENNY. which guy?

KY. you know
　　the one who played the Bad Guy

DENNY. Really?
　　You saw him?

KY. yep

DENNY. like just on the Street?

KY. well that's what it's like in LA, Squirt
　　Everyday
　　Movie Stars
　　Everywhere All The Time

DENNY. then how come I haven't seen one yet?

KY. maybe you'll see one this weekend

DENNY. you think so?

KY. Sure

　　Denny imagines who he might see
　　Pause

KY. so
　　You guys Win?

　　Denny shrugs

KY. Is that a Yes or a No?

　　Denny shrugs

KY. Your Mother manage to find a Job yet?

DENNY. What do You think?

KY. well I noticed the eBay Thing stopped –

DENNY. nah
　　She just got a new Credit Card

KY. When?

DENNY. When I told her you were Spying on her

KY. We Share an Account

DENNY. Whatever

KY. Who in their Right Mind would give that Woman a
　　Credit Card?

Denny shrugs

DENNY. eBay

> *Ky shakes his head*
> *He looks at the Dash and sees a CD*

KY. Were you gonna put my CD away or just leave it like
that?

DENNY. I didn't put it there

KY. It's gonna get Scratched like that, Denny
you know this

DENNY. I didn't do it

KY. How would you like it if I treated your Property like
that?
Huh?
come on Give it to me

> *Denny plays a quick game of keep away with his Dad*
> *then hands Ky the CD and pops it in*

> *A Woman's Voice coos to Acoustic Guitar Back-up*

> *It's reminiscent of a live musician in a cheesy LA coffee shop*
> *Music that's followed by polite applause*
> *Music that's anathema to a young boy's ears*
> *It Gnaws at Denny's Soul*
> *We can see it on his face*

> *A long moment of Ky's music*
> *Ky taps the steering wheel to the Beat*

> *Finally*
> *Denny speaks up*

DENNY. Who Is this?

KY. You like it?

> *Denny Squirms*

DENNY. Since when do you listen to Chick Rock?
I thought you were obsessed with Coldplay

KY. Maybe your Dad's Taste In Music is a little more Rockin
than you Think

DENNY. Whatever

Can we listen to something else?

Ky doesn't respond

His Chick Rock plays

Denny rolls his eyes
He rummages through his sports bag
and removes an iPod with an attached iTrip

He Stops his Father's CD

KY. Denny

DENNY. What?

KY. I was listening to that

DENNY. It sounds like Sheryl Crow on Crack

KY. It's a Good Album

DENNY. Yeah for Fags

KY. Hey!

Denny moves to eject the CD

KY. Denny

DENNY. What?

KY. You ask someone / before you

DENNY. I did ask

KY. and did I give you Permission?

DENNY. you didn't say anything / so I just took it as a yes

KY. that's right I

No

that's not

When someone doesn't respond that doesn't mean
you can –

DENNY. Fine

can I put something else on?

Ky reaches for the stereo and Defiantly Presses Play
Ky's Chick Rock plays

Denny turns towards the window

DENNY. I so wish you weren't my Dad

KY. Excuse me?

You wanna Enunciate?

DENNY. I said: I So Wish You Weren't My Dad

KY. Hey!

Don't say something you don't Mean

Denny mutters to himself

DENNY. cock fiend

The Low Hum of a Car in Motion

KY. so

You guys Win?

Denny shrugs

KY. Is that a Yes or a No?

Denny shrugs
Ky shakes his head

KY. How's the Job Hunt going?

Small Pause

KY. you know

I think they're gonna find those WMDs before that
woman finds a Job

Ky is Very Proud of this joke
He smiles to himself and nudges Denny

KY. You like that?

Eh?

Your Dad can be a Pretty Funny Guy, huh?

He nudges Denny again
He makes Silly noises and Playfully Nudges his Son
He might even Tickle him a Little

KY. Wockawockawockawockawockawockawockawock-
awockawockawockawocka

Denny Laughs a Bunch
Ky Laughs a Bunch
Lots and Lots of Laughs

KY. Hey

what do you think about coming to Live with your Dad
for a while, Huh?

we can Start in the Summer so you don't miss School

maybe make it a More Permanent Thing down the
Road

and hey who knows

you might even see a Movie Star

DENNY. you think so?

KY. Nyah

Nyah

Hey, Wise Guy

Nyah

Here's looking at you, Kiddo

Nyah

DENNY. what are doing?

KY. what do you mean what am I doing?

It's a Classic

Nyah Nyah

DENNY. stop

Ky laughs
He tickles his Son

KY. so what do you say?

you wanna come live with your Old Man?

DENNY. Mom says you didn't want Custody

KY. I never said that –

DENNY. She said that You said if you had Custody you'd
never get any Ass –

KY. Look

your Mother needs to stop Inventing Lies about me
and start Waiting Tables

Pause

KY. you know, Squirt

you're the Reason I wake up in the Morning

DENNY. I'm sure –

KY. I mean it
   you're the Sun and Moon and Stars

DENNY. Wow
   that's maybe the Gayest thing you've ever Said

KY. well it's the Truth

DENNY. then how come you never come to my Club games?

KY. well if your Mother would get off her ass and find a Job
   maybe I wouldn't have to Work Saturdays

DENNY. Sun and Moon my Nuts

KY. Denny
   listen to me
   I'm your Father and
   and I love you Very Much
   okay?
   and I'd love nothing more than to have you come Live
   with me
   but I'm not gonna Push You, okay?
   because I can recognize
   that you're both Old enough and Smart enough
   to Make Your Own Decisions

DENNY. you really think that?

KY. Damn Right

DENNY. Mom says I can barely wipe my own Ass

KY. well your Mother's just scared of losing her Little Boy
   whereas your Dad
   see
   your Dad's excited to see you become a Man
   huh?
   huh?
   What do you say Manly Man?

   Ky smacks his chest
   Denny smiles a little

   Pause

DENNY. so um

how's Work?

Ky glances at his Son
He's surprised by the question
Maybe even a little touched

KY. It's Good

DENNY. Is your New Office better than the one in Orange
County?

KY. It's uh
well it's definitely Bigger
lots of New Faces
and my New Boss
Fred
he's pretty Great
Smart
Funny
yeah
Fred's uh
Really Great
and well
the employees in LA are Certainly more Eclectic than
the ones in Orange County

DENNY. what's Eclectic mean?

KY. oh come on
how Old are you?

DENNY. Sorry

KY. it means Diverse
like
like something that's drawn from a Large Spectrum

DENNY. what's a Spectrum?

KY. Jesus Denny
it's uh
like a Rainbow
you know
something with lots of Different Colors

DENNY. oh

so Eclectic means Gay

KY. no –

DENNY. Is Fred gay?

KY. I don't know, Denny

DENNY. so he's Gay

KY. I don't know

DENNY. Is that why Mom dropped you?

cuz you went Gay for Fred?

KY. Denny –

DENNY. You know

it's like a new Millennium or whatever, Dad

so don't feel like you have to Deny Your Gayness

KY. I'm not – !

Okay

You know what

I'm choosing Not to Feed into

What is Essentially

Your Mother's Negativity manifesting itself in Your
Behavior

Okay?

Denny shivers
He reaches into the backseat and grabs Ky's coat
Underneath the Jacket are a Briefcase and a Stack of Papers

Denny begins to slip on the Jacket

KY. What do you think you're doing?

DENNY. It's like Siberia in here

KY. Hey watch the Papers, Denny –

okay Give me the Coat

DENNY. Why?

KY. cuz I don't wanna go into Work tomorrow smelling like
a Jock Strap

how would you like it if I treated your Property like that?

come on Give me the Coat

Denny holds out the coat
Ky takes it
Smells it
Ugh

KY. Jesus Christ, Denny
   I just had this Dry Cleaned

DENNY. so get it Dry Cleaned again

KY. Dry Cleaning costs Money

DENNY. so?
   it's not like you're spending any on Child Support

KY. okay
   you know what
   No Playstation this Weekend

DENNY. What?

KY. You heard me

DENNY. That's so not fair

KY. Tough Shit

DENNY. Since when did you decide to join the Taliban

KY. oh You want me to donate your Playstation to Charity?
   Just keep talking
   I'm sure Juan Ricardo and his sixteen brothers and sis-
   ters can't wait to get their hands on the New Tony Hawk

   Denny curls up
   He mutters to himself

DENNY. I so wish you weren't my Dad

   Pause
   Denny pouts

KY. You think I like punishing you?
   Believe me I wish I didn't Have To
   but someone's got to teach you some Discipline
   cuz you're clearly not learning any At Home

   Ky neatly lays the coat out in the backseat
   while watching the road

He drives

KY. The woman's too busy Trolling the Orange County sin-
gles scene to raise her Son properly

Ky shakes his head in Disgust

KY. yeah I see where she spends her money
Wet Seal
Forever 21
You know who shops at places like that?
Women looking to get Laid

You might want to Remind her that we still share a
MasterCard Account

Small Pause

KY. you know
there was a time when I wanted to hold those Hands
for the Rest of my Life

Ky shakes his head

KY. When's the last time she cooked for you, Huh?
no Lemme guess
Sophomore Year?
Right
She doesn't have Time to provide you a Home-cooked
Meal anymore

These days
She just drops some In-N-Out in front of you
shoves some Condoms into her Purse
and runs out the Door in her Fuck-Me Boots

am I right?

Ky glances at Denny
No response
Denny pouts

KY. well when she Does start Dating Again
Some Lucky Prick's in for one Big Disappointment
Now don't get me wrong

I mean your Mother's a Beautiful Woman
an Amazing Woman
but a Man can only take so much Anger and Sloth
you know?

Denny pouts

KY. I hope you Realize who you're adopting this Attitude Problem from
God
everything's a Fight with her
Every Tiny Little Thing
mah mah mah mah mah mah
and once she Starts
psh

Ky drives

KY. She manage to find a Job yet?

Denny shrugs

KY. Is that a Yes or a No?

Denny shrugs
Ky drives

KY. well if she thinks I'm paying for your college on top of everything else
she's Out of Her Mind
Just remember
if you end up at a JC next year
you only have her to Thank

Ky drives

KY. She ever tell you about all the Blow she did in the Eighties?
Oh Yeah
A real Winner your Mom
She was Coked Up on our Wedding Day for Christ's Sake

yeah
She'd complain if we spent a little money going out to
Eat twice a month
but the next thing you know she's bent over the Coffee
Table with a Straw up her nose Snorting that stuff like
it Grows on Trees

Ky drives

KY. I tell you, Squirt
Nothing in the World could get your Dad to walk down
That Aisle again

Ky drives

KY. You know if she's dating Anyone?

Ky drives

KY. Women
I'm telling ya
Men should know better
but They Suck our Dicks once in a while and we let em
Get Away with Murder
am I right?

Ky glances at Denny
Denny presses his face against the window

KY. I guess you're uh
still a little Too Young Huh?

Ky reaches out
He squeezes Denny's shoulder

Denny picks at the Window
and for a second
it seems as if the Tint
has changed Color

a Strange Shade of Maroon

but before we're sure it was ever there at all
it's Gone

KY. you know
>When I was your age
>There was this Girl
>Samantha McAllister
>Long blond curls
>Green eyes
>Kind of a Dog to be Honest but she had a Pretty Good Ass for a Twelve Year-Old
>Samantha McAllister
>Jesus Christ
>First girl I ever kissed
>
>*Ky smiles*

KY. Get this
>The first time I kiss her
>I think she's Pregnant
>
>at Twelve Years Old
>Can you Imagine?
>
>Those Nuns
>Let me Tell You
>They did a number on Me
>
>you uh
>You know how a Girl Gets Pregnant?
>
>*Ky pinches Denny*
>*Denny flinches*

DENNY. Yeah

KY. And you know how a Girl Doesn't Get Pregnant?

DENNY. Dad –

KY. hey the last thing I need is to be a Grandfather
>so I just want to make sure
>that when the Time Comes
>you're Fully Prepared
>Okay?
>When I was your age

all we had were Magazines
But now you Kids
You got the Internet
and that's uh
That's a Great Resource to have around
you know
if you've got Questions

Pause

KY. Hey
if you're ever Curious
I know a few websites
and if you Want
you can uh
use my passwords –

DENNY. I'm fine

Pause

KY. there's only One Thing I want to Warn you about
okay?
and it's Important
so Listen Up

Denny keeps his face pressed against the Window

KY. now Most Guys think if you Pull Out before you Ejaculate you're in the Clear
but what they Don't Know is
that well before Climax
the Erect Penis releases a tiny batch of Sperm that's
even more potent than The Big One
It's called Pre-Cum
and Pre-Cum
lemme tell you Squirt
Pre-Cum
that's the Stuff that'll Fuck Ya

Pause
Denny remains Firmly pressed against the Window

KY. so
    Anyone got your Attention?

DENNY. What do you mean Attention?

Ky tousles Denny's hair
Playful
Fatherly

KY. you know
    You got your eye on any Pussy?

DENNY. Girls don't even talk to me
    okay?

More Tousling

KY. Come on Big Guy
    Can't talk Pussy with your Old Man?

DENNY. Stop saying that

KY. What?

DENNY. the P word

KY. there's nothing Wrong with the P Word

DENNY. it's Disrespectful

KY. says Who?

DENNY. my Girlfriend

Ky beams a little

KY. oh a Girlfriend?
    I thought Girls didn't talk to you

DENNY. well they kinda do Now

KY. When'd this happen?

Denny shrugs

DENNY. After I started Club

KY. What's her Name?

DENNY. Monique

KY. Monique huh?
    Look at You
    Big Pimpin

Small Pause

KY. You uh
   You get your hands Fishy yet?

DENNY. Huh?

KY. You know
   Fishy

   Ky flashes three fingers
   Denny gives Ky a Strange Look

KY. come on Big Pimpin
   you can tell Pimp Daddy

DENNY. Dad –

KY. What?

DENNY. Amber's Catholic so she barely even lets me Kiss
   her

KY. I'm warning you, Squirt
   Be Careful with those Catholic Girls
   They're nothing but a Recipe for Blue Balls

   Denny doesn't Get It

KY. I uh
   I guess you're still a little too young Huh?

   Denny shrugs

DENNY. I guess

KY. You guess?

DENNY. Yeah
   I guess

   Denny stares out the window

KY. What do you mean You Guess?

DENNY. Nothing

   Small Pause

KY. Have you uh –

   Denny smiles
   but he hides it against the window

DENNY. I don't want to talk about it

KY. Are you smiling?

DENNY. No

KY. You Have

You little Son of a Bitch

Ky tousles Denny's hair

KY. Wockawockawockawockawockawockawockawock-
awockawockawockawocka

DENNY. Cut it out!

Ky stops
He smiles

KY. Does this Lucky Young Lady have a Name?

DENNY. Dad

KY. Well?

DENNY. Cynthia

KY. Cynthia huh?

DENNY. Yeah

KY. Look at You

Big Pimpin

Ky smacks Denny's chest Hard

KY. Hey what do you Bench these days anyway?

DENNY. I don't Bench

KY. Why not?

DENNY. cuz it's not Healthy for someone my age

Coach Ying says I shouldn't start benching until I'm at
least Fourteen

KY. Oh Come On

that's horse shit

Hey I tell you what

I got a Weight Room set up in the apartment

when we get to Silver Lake we'll put you on the Bench

Help you get your mind off that little What's-Her-Face –

DENNY. Her name's Sarah and I really Liked her

KY. well Sarah's gotta be the Dumbest Girl in the World

DENNY. She's in every AP class, Dad

KY. I'm just saying

something's Seriously Wrong with her if she dumped a Great Guy like you

DENNY. I'm sure –

KY. okay Maybe you've adopted a little too much of your Mom's Sensitivity

but Seriously, Squirt

One day you're gonna make some Lucky Lady Very Very Happy

Denny smiles a little

DENNY. You think so?

KY. I know so

you're the Sun and Moon and Stars

Small Pause

DENNY. um

how's Work?

Ky's surprised by the Question
Maybe even a little Touched

KY. it's Good

you know I think Fred's gonna give me that Raise

DENNY. that's Cool

KY. yeah it is Cool

Ky smiles at his Son

KY. come on

lemme get you set up on that Bench, Huh?

Ky smacks Denny on the chest twice
Hard
Open-palmed
Fatherly

Denny recoils

DENNY. Nah

KY. Come on

DENNY. Coach Ying says / I'm not supposed –

KY. is Coach Ying your Father?

DENNY. no

KY. and who knows what's Best for you?
   Your Father
   or some Japanese Meathead?

DENNY. he knows what he's talking about –

KY. Yeah?
   What makes him so Qualified?

DENNY. He used to play for the Galaxy

KY. The Galaxy?
   What's that
   a String Quartet?
   Wockawockawockawockawockawockawocka

Ky Nudges Denny
Not so Much with the Laughs

DENNY. The Los Angeles Galaxy
   The Professional Soccer Team

Ky shakes his head

KY. When did they start playing Soccer anyway?
   I mean Come On
   They just figured out how to swing a Bat for Christ's
   sake
   huh?
   huh?

   ah Lighten Up
   your Dad's just having a little fun

Pause
The Low Hum of a Car in Motion
Denny watches the landscape zoom by

DENNY. Dad?

KY. Yeah Squirt?

DENNY. Do we get to go home soon?

> *Ky drives*
> *He glances at his Son*

KY. Not yet, Pal

DENNY. Dad

> I'm Scared
> What's wrong, Dad?

KY. Hey

> you gotta Trust Me, okay?
> we'll get there Soon
> but first
> first we gotta make sure that it's Safe

DENNY. but how do we know when it's Safe?

> *Ky checks the rearview*
>
> *and the Car starts to Shake*
> *it shakes Hard and Fast*
> *then*
> *it Stops*
> *and it's like nothing ever happened*

KY. You guys win?

> *Denny shrugs*

KY. You score any Goals?

DENNY. I play Sweeper

KY. So?

DENNY. so Sweeper's Defense

> and Coach Ying's not Japanese by the way
> his Grandparents immigrated from Beijing
> and his Mom's like 100% Irish

> *Pause*

DENNY. oh my God

> there's an In-N-Out Right There
> come on, Dad

KY. I told you we have Dinner Plans

DENNY. what kind of Dinner Plans?

KY. it's a Surprise

DENNY. Surprises are Gay

KY. okay Fine!

we're gonna Barbecue, okay?

Are you Happy?

I thought that'd be a Fun Surprise since you Love Barbecue so Much but now it's Ruined

DENNY. I hate Barbecue

KY. you Love Barbecue

DENNY. it takes too long

KY. well you Loved Barbecue when you were Little

You remember us Grilling on the Porch together in the Summer?

Just you and me

the Grillmeisters

DENNY. No

KY. well you Loved It

Ky softens
He gets Nostalgic

KY. I remember

I'd Pick You Up so you could see the Meat

and I mean you're Little Little

and I'd Say

"Denny How do we know when to Flip The Meat?"

and You'd Say

You'd Say:

"The Juice, Dad!"

over and over

"The Juice!"

"The Juice!"

"The Juice, Dad!"

Ky Smiles Big
He pinches Denny a Little
Denny Flinches

KY. eh?

you remember that, Grillmeister?

Denny watches the landscape zoom by

DENNY. why'd you move to Silver Lake?

Small Pause

DENNY. Dad?

KY. Why don't you turn on the Game?
Huh?
Come on
they're playing the Giants
You Love the Giants

Denny rolls his eyes
He pushes a Button on the Stereo
He fiddles with the dial
and for a moment we hear a Baseball Game
but very quickly the Baseball Game becomes
the sound of a Man and Boy's voices beneath a Stereophonic
hiss
as if they're coming from very far away

BOY. Coach Denny –

MAN. Yeah Squirt?

BOY. You think this team's gonna be better than our
team?

MAN. now what makes you ask something like that?

BOY. cuz they're from LA
and like
everything from LA's better

MAN. oh Come On
we're gonna Kick Their Butts

A Hiss

BOY. my Mom says "thanks" by the way

MAN. well tell her if you ever need a Ride again
I'm more than happy to help

A Hiss

BOY. Coach Denny?

MAN. yeah Squirt?

BOY. how far do we have till the field?

MAN. You gotta be patient

BOY. but how far?

MAN. why don't you turn on the Radio, Squirt?

*Ky Angrily hits a button on the stereo
the Radio clicks off*

KY. Son of a –

DENNY. How far do we have?

*Ky sighs
He turns his Chick Rock back up*

KY. we're near Tustin

DENNY. So
how far?

KY. You really gotta learn to be more patient

DENNY. Is it at least gonna Snow this weekend?
I've never seen Snow before

KY. Denny it's LA

DENNY. So?

Denny looks out the window

DENNY. Can Chris come over again next week?

KY. mm I don't think so, Buddy

DENNY. why not?
I thought you liked him

KY. I do I do
he's very nice

DENNY. so why can't he come over again?

KY. Denny
　　look
　　Chris
　　he's uh
　　well he's a Messy Kid

DENNY. no he's not!

KY. Denny I know he's your friend –

DENNY. my best friend –

KY. but all he did the Entire Weekend
　　was sit in front of the TV in his underwear eating Dori-
　　tos
　　did you see what he did to your Playstation?
　　I mean those controllers were just Caked in Gunk

DENNY. so?

KY. so
　　it's pretty clear his father didn't teach him any man-
　　ners

DENNY. yeah he has

KY. I really don't think so, Pal

DENNY. his dad teaches him all kinds of things

KY. Oh yeah?
　　Such As?

DENNY. he plays soccer with Chris all the time

KY. And?

DENNY. And you've never even played with me Once

　　Ky is Startled
　　Wounded
　　but before his Son can notice
　　Ky buries it

KY. okay
　　well
　　hey I tell you what
　　when we get to LA
　　we'll

you know
Run Some Drills
maybe play a little One-On-One
huh?
just you and me

Ky squeezes Denny's shoulder

Denny shrugs with a slight smile

KY. Nyah Nyah
how's that, Big Guy?
Think you can score some Goals on your Old Man?
wockawockawockawocka

Tousle Tousle

Denny's smile vanishes

DENNY. I play Sweeper

KY. so?

DENNY. so Sweeper's Defense
they don't score goals

Pause

KY. Hey why don't you eat something?

DENNY. I'm not hungry

KY. Oh Now you're not hungry?

DENNY. What'd you get?

*Denny leans forward and picks up the Bag
it's full of Food*

KY. Double-Double Animal Style

DENNY. Does it have Tomatoes?

Denny sifts through the Bag

KY. I had them make it how you like it

Denny removes a Burger

DENNY. Are these Pickles?

KY. What?
You don't like pickles now?

DENNY. Uh uh

KY. Since when?

> *Denny shrugs*

KY. Well pick them off

DENNY. I'm not really hungry anyway

KY. Come on

DENNY. I don't even like In-N-Out

KY. oh please

> You love In-N-Out

DENNY. it's Really Bad for You, Dad

KY. says Who?

DENNY. says Everyone

> Mom brings me Caesar Salad Wraps from Jack-in-the
> Box after my Games Now
>
> they're really Tasty and they only have like Six Carbs
> and Five Grams of Fat
>
> and besides
>
> In-N-Out's all Christian

KY. What?

DENNY. Like on the bottoms of the cups and inside the
> burger wrappers
>
> they've got like Scripture
>
> I'm serious
>
> Look

> *Denny peels back the Wrapper*

DENNY. See?

> Nahum 1:7
>
> Like
>
> what the hell's Nahum 1:7
>
> and what's it doing on my Double-Double?
>
> It like violates Separation of Church and State or some-
> thing

> *Denny drops the Burger back in the Bag*

Pause

KY. The Lord is good
a Stronghold in the Day of Trouble
and He knows those who trust in Him

Denny gives his father an odd look
Ky smiles some

KY. Nahum 1:7
The Lord is good
a Stronghold in the Day of Trouble –

DENNY. yeah okay

KY. I was an altar boy when I was your age –

DENNY. yeah I know –

KY. okay well
You pick up a few things

DENNY. Whatever
Just stop
Christian stuff freaks me out

KY. oh yeah?

DENNY. Kinda

KY. Why's that?

DENNY. cuz at School
I'm always just tryin to chill with my friends and stuff
and the Church Freaks come up to me and say like
"do you feel Jesus in your heart?"
and I'm like
"No"
and they're like
"Do you want to?"
and I'm like
"Uh get the hell away from me"
and they're like
"You shouldn't say hell – "
and I'm like
"Peace, Church Freak"

Denny watches the Landscape zoom by
Pause

KY. you know, Squirt
I'm Christian

DENNY. yeah
when you were little

KY. no
what I mean is
I uh
I opened myself up
and
Rediscovered Christ

Denny turns away from the window
He looks Horrified

DENNY. No Way

KY. yeah way

DENNY. So do you go to church and like Sing and Eat
Wafers and Drink Wine and Pray and Stuff?

Ky nods
Denny comes to a Horrifying Realization

DENNY. oh my god –

KY. What's the matter?

DENNY. Is this CHRISTIAN Chick Rock?

A moment of Ky's Chick Rock
The words Jesus, Lord, and Savior are Eerily Clear

KY. There are Christian themes, sure, but I wouldn't call
it –

Denny lets out a small, sickened moan
and curls up towards the Window

KY. Hey
Denny

the Tint on the Windows change Color
and what begins as a Strange Shade of Maroon

transforms into the color of every phase of the Sky
from Dawn to Twilight
until the Window is
once again
just a Window

KY. you know what, Pal
it might seem Silly now
but Someday
Someday something really Bad's gonna happen to you
and you're gonna need help
Big Time Help
Like more help than Me or Your Mom or Anyone Else
can provide
believe me
if I had it my way
you'd be Kept Safe your Whole Life
but there's only so much your Dad can do
so when that Day comes, Kiddo
well
Mark my Words
when that Day comes
you're gonna want Something Very Strong to Hold
Onto

Ky sighs
He smiles

KY. the Lord is Good
a Stronghold in the Day of Trouble
and He knows those who Trust in Him

Denny reaches into his pocket and removes a cell phone
He presses his forehead against the glass and futzes with it

An obnoxious noise blares from the phone
followed shortly by another obnoxious noise

Ky can't tell if it's Machinery Clanging or Cats Dying
but whatever it is

It's Gnawing at his Soul

KY. denny

DENNY. What?

KY. You ever hear of noise pollution?

DENNY. I need a new ring tone
    Chill out

KY. What's wrong with the ring tone you have?

DENNY. uh
    I've had it for over a week

    Ring tone

KY. You know that costs money

    Denny shrugs
    Ring tone

KY. Your Mother find a Job yet?

DENNY. Does your girlfriend live in Silver Lake?

KY. Girlfriend?

DENNY. Does she?

KY. Hey –

DENNY. Is that why you moved there?

    Ring tone

KY. I don't –
    Who told you that?
    Your mother?

DENNY. No
    Mom says you moved to Silver Lake so you could tag
    Twenty-Something Poontang

    Ring tone

KY. Okay
    That's Enough

DENNY. What?

KY. The Ring Tones
    That's it

You're finished

DENNY. I'm almost done

Ring tone

KY. The ring tone you have is Fine

DENNY. well I want a New One

and it's my right as an American to have what I want

What are you like the Ring Tone Gestapo?

KY. Denny

I'm your father and I'm putting the Kibosh on the ring
tones This Instant

DENNY. Kibosh?

KY. Yeah Kibosh

DENNY. I didn't realize the Gestapo was Jewish

KY. Put It Away!

Denny glares at his father
and shoves the Cell Phone into his pocket as he mutters to
himself

DENNY. I so wish you weren't my Dad

KY. Excuse me?

Pause

KY. Denny

I want you to hear me on something

and it's Very Important

so Listen Up:

No One

I mean No One

Will Ever Replace Your Mom

Nothing in the World could get your Dad to walk down
That Aisle again

You got me?

I can't

I can't even believe she'd say something like that to
you

She likes to Run Her Mouth so much
What else does she tell you?
Huh?
She ever tell you the story about the Guy she was
engaged to in College?
She ever tell you That One?
oh It's Good
The Poor Guy catches her in the Shower with two of
his Roommates
and Get this:
One of them ain't a Man

now Out of respect for your Mom I'm not gonna go
into detail about what she was or wasn't Discovered
Doing
so I'll just leave that one to your Imagination

Ky softens
He glances at Denny

KY. Denny

Denny pouts

KY. Denny
hey I'm talking to you

Pause

KY. fine
if you're not gonna Respond
then I'm just gonna have to make a Face
yeah
you've Really Done It Now
well let's see
What Face Is It Gonna Be?

DENNY. don't

KY. what's that?
you want me to make the Monkey Face?

DENNY. no

KY. okay
> watch out
> here it comes
> here comes the Monkey Face

> *Ky makes the Monkey face*
> *it's Ridiculous*
> *Denny glances over*
> *he giggles a little*

KY. eep eep eep

DENNY. stop

KY. well if you keep being Mad
> you leave me No Choice
> now what do you want next?
> you want the Turtle Face?

DENNY. dad

KY. here comes the Turtle Face

> *Ky makes the Turtle face*
> *Denny can't help but giggle*

KY. heeeelllooooo deeeeeeennyy

> *Denny suppresses a smile*

DENNY. it's the same as your Monkey face except you Talk Slow

> *Ky keeps at it*

KY. aaaare yoooou caaaaalliiiing meeee Uuuuunooooooriginal?

> *Ky laughs*
> *Denny laughs*
> *Lots of laughs*

> *then*
> *Long Silence*

> *Denny sneaks a look at Ky*
> *for a Second*

we see the kind of Awe a Son has for his Father
maybe it betrays itself in the Eyes
or in the slightest hint of a Smile
but just as quickly as it surfaces
Denny buries it

DENNY. you're So Weird

Ky smiles

KY. you know what Fred had me do Today?
Shred Sales Reports
you believe that?
I say to him
I say: Fred
a Man my Age shouldn't be spending his Saturdays
Shredding Sales Reports
that's what Temps are for
but does Fred give a / shit?

DENNY. no

KY. No!
that's right
so there I am shredding Sales Reports on a Saturday
instead of spending Time with my Son

Can you believe that?

I tell you, Squirt
Enjoy these Years while you can
cuz pretty soon
Life's nothin but Work Work Work Work Work

Denny doodles against the window
but as he does
the Tint changes Color
and we can see the imprint of Denny's Doodles on every
window in the Car
they are Strange Shapes
they come to Life

the Squiggles and Static of a Child's Imagination

fill the Interior for a moment
then Vanish

DENNY. okay for real

Can we listen to My Music now?

KY. no

DENNY. Why Not?

KY. because that Hip Hop Crap your Mom buys you is Totally Inappropriate for a Child

DENNY. I'm a Teenager

KY. A teenager's still a Child

DENNY. I already have my driver's permit

KY. oh

A Driver's Permit

what's That supposed to mean?

DENNY. it Means that in a few months I Can Drive which means I'm practically an Adult

KY. Yeah well

If you think you're getting behind the wheel before you're Eighteen

you're Dreaming

DENNY. ffff

Like you have any say in the matter

Ky grins a little

KY. I hate to break it to you, Squirt

but your mother and I

before we made anything official

the two of us had a little Sit Down at Outback Steakhouse

DENNY. So?

KY. So

it's important for a family to set aside a Neutral Public Space

for the sole purpose of negotiation

and Outback Steakhouse

is traditionally
for our family
That Space
Your mother and I worked out a number of details
about your future we both felt were in your best inter-
est
And it just so happens the age you start to drive was
one of them
and the Agreement was Eighteen
not Sixteen
not Seventeen
Eighteen
End of Story

DENNY. Then how come she's gonna buy me a car when I
turn Sixteen?

KY. She can't afford to buy you a car

DENNY. She can now

KY. Oh really?

DENNY. Yeah really
she's got a Job

KY. oh She finally got a Job?

DENNY. yeah

KY. Well good for her
She waitressing?

DENNY. No
She works for some Company in Irvine

KY. oh Yeah?

DENNY. yeah

KY. Doing what?

DENNY. I didn't ask

KY. Why not?

DENNY. cuz all I need to know is she's gonna buy me a Car

KY. okay

DENNY. your mother's Job

Whatever it is
there's no way In Hell it pays Well Enough for her to
afford a New Car

DENNY. She already bought one for herself

Pause

KY. She bought a car?

DENNY. Uh huh
a Pass-At
It's really cool too
I mean
it's got a Spoiler and Everything

KY. Passat

DENNY. What?

KY. Passat
It's pronounced –
okay
wait
She bought herself a Car?

DENNY. I told you
She got a job

KY. I know, Denny
but what confuses me is
Your mother
Okay
Your mother is a Beautiful Woman
an Amazing Woman
but
between you and me, Squirt
she doesn't
well
Her skills are not particularly Marketable
I mean are you sure she's not
I don't know

Seeing someone?

DENNY. god

KY. What?

DENNY. Man she's so right about you
You think she's a Ditz, huh?

KY. I never said Ditz –

DENNY. you basically did just now –

KY. Did I say Ditz?
No
what I said was –

DENNY. she says you've always thought she was a Ditz –

KY. No
Denny no
what I'm saying is
your Mother
your mother is –
She's a very Unique Person
with very Unique Abilities
They're just abilities that
in this world
in this Economy
seem to me
Difficult to Market

DENNY. Well either way
She's gonna buy me a car
and you know what?
It's gonna have way more Legroom than yours

Ky seethes

KY. you know
She always Insisted on cluttering her life with Extrava-
gancies
For Years she Bitched about the Andersons' porch
The Woman wouldn't shut up about it
I mean

the fact I'd just put in a Swimming Pool didn't matter
oh no
All she could talk about was that Goddamn Porch
Day and Night
Drove me up the Wall
but what'd your Dad do, huh?
what'd he do?
He built
your Mom
a Porch

I tell you, Squirt
You think you know what it takes to Love someone and
then –
fffff

Small Pause

DENNY. I thought those Mexican guys built the Porch

KY. What Mexican guys?

DENNY. Those two Mexican guys who were around for a
while
Ricky and Miguel or whatever
They were always telling Jokes about Butt Holes
I thought they built it

Ky mutters under his breath

KY. a Passat

you know
as a Christian
I have to question the Example she's setting for You

Denny looks out the Window

DENNY. Dad –

KY. She find a Job?

DENNY. Dad –

KY. or does she expect Me to foot the Bill for that Club
Team?

DENNY. Hey –

KY. What?

DENNY. Is it Safe yet?

> *Ky adjusts the Rearview*
> *the Car starts to Shake again*
> *It Shakes as if it's Bounding down a Dirt Road*
>
> *and for a moment*
> *we can see*
> *what we think might be*
> *Pine Trees*
> *flying past the windows*

KY. Not yet, Squirt

DENNY. Where are we going, Dad?

KY. Everything's gonna be fine

DENNY. I wanna call Mom

KY. there's no need to Involve Your Mother

DENNY. but if there's Trouble –

KY. Hey there's No Trouble
this is just something for us Guys

DENNY. I wanna go Home, Dad
why can't I go Home?

KY. well
you're gonna have to Trust Your Dad on this one, okay
Pal?

> *Ky adjusts the rearview*
> *and the Shaking Stops as if nothing ever happened*

KY. hey
you know who you're starting to look like?

DENNY. who?

KY. your Grandfather

DENNY. I do?

> *Ky nods*

KY. you know I've got some Pictures of him at the apartment you can even see your Dad when he was a Kid

DENNY. no way

KY. yeah way

DENNY. what were you like then?

KY. mm

I guess I was a lot like you

Ky pokes Denny
Denny looks sorely disappointed by this revelation

DENNY. really?

KY. yep

he tousles Denny's hair

KY. you know what Fred had me do Today?
Hole Punch Sales Reports
You believe that?
I tell him:
A Man My Age
you're gonna give me Carpal Tunnel
but does Fred give a / shit?

DENNY. no

KY. No!
that's right
So there I am Hole Punching on a Saturday instead of
spending Time with my Son
I tell you, Squirt
Work Work Work Work Work

the Sound of a Man and Boy's voices beneath a Stereophonic
hiss
like they're coming from very far away

> **MAN.** I tell you, Squirt
> Work Work Work Work Work
> **BOY.** Coach Denny –
> **MAN.** yeah Kiddo?
> **BOY.** why doesn't your Son play for our team?
> **MAN.** cuz I don't have a Son, pal

BOY. do you have a Daughter?

MAN. nope

BOY. but you're Married, right?

MAN. 'fraid not

BOY. are you at least Divorced?

A Hiss

BOY. you know
since my Dad left
my Mom goes on a lot of Dates

MAN. oh yeah?

BOY. they're all Jerks though

MAN. who?

BOY. her Boyfriends
they all Smile too much

MAN. maybe they're Happy

BOY. well all they do is make my mom Cry
you think she'll ever find someone who can
make her Happy?

MAN. these things take time, Pal

BOY. she told me she thinks you're Handsome
do you think she's Handsome?

MAN. your mom's uh
Very Nice

BOY. she says you have Nice Calves
like the soccer players on the Galaxy
do you play Soccer anymore?

A Hiss

BOY. Why not?

A Hiss

BOY. whoa
What's That?

MAN. what's what?

BOY. That

> right there
> is that a Mountain? –

Denny spots something in the distance

KY. hey
> What would you think about coming to live with your
> Dad for a while, huh?

DENNY. What is that?

KY. we could start in the Summer so you don't have to Miss
> School

DENNY. Is that a Mountain?

KY. Denny, I'm talking to you –

DENNY. I didn't know there were Mountains in Anaheim

KY. That's not a Mountain

DENNY. what is it?

KY. the Matterhorn

DENNY. it's not a Real Mountain?

KY. It's a Ride

DENNY. but is that Real Snow on top?

KY. It's Disneyland, Squirt
> None of it's Real

DENNY. Can we go and see the Snow?
> I've never seen Snow before

KY. Did you hear a word I said?!

Ky calms himself
he becomes surprisingly open

KY. look
> it's just
> your Dad misses you, Buddy
> I mean these Weekends are Great
> they're So Great
> to be Honest
> they're kinda what gets your Dad through the rest of
> the week

but they're uh
they're not really Enough, you know?

so what do you say, huh?
you wanna come live with your old man?

DENNY. If I came to live with you
would your Girlfriend live with us?

KY. What Girlfriend?

DENNY. The one you cheated on Mom with
Her name's Darcy, right?
Darcy the Starbucks Barista

KY. Did your mother tell you that?

DENNY. It's true, isn't it?

KY. Denny
Your mother was Not –
We were supposed to tell you Together

DENNY. Oh yeah?
When?

KY. When you're Older

DENNY. It's not like I'm a Kid

KY. Believe it or not You Are –

DENNY. no I'm Not
a kid can't Drive –

KY. well you're still too Young to Understand –

DENNY. Yeah whatever
I Understand just fine
You banged a Barista
and when Mom found out
she Dumped you

KY. That's Not –
Okay
You have to understand a few things, Denny
First of all
Darcy was not a Barista
she was a Musician

and Second
your Mother signed an Agreement –

DENNY. Is Darcy your girlfriend still?
Is that why you moved to Silver Lake?
To like
Be with Her?

KY. no

DENNY. then What?

KY. I told you, Pal
your Dad got a Job

DENNY. yeah a Blow Job

KY. Denny!
look
your Dad
your Dad made a Mistake
a Big Mistake
and what happened there
well
that's between your Dad and your Mom and God –

DENNY. and me

KY. yes
and You

DENNY. and the Barista

KY. she was not – !
you're Right
you're absolutely right
but the fact of the matter is
your Mom's not telling you the whole Story

DENNY. oh did you cheat on Darcy too?

KY. alright
this Woman your Mom told you about
Darcy
it's over between us, okay?

DENNY. oh yeah?
prove it

KY. okay okay Fine
      after the Divorce
      I told her about You
      and That Was It, okay?
      She wanted out

      There you go
      that's the Truth
      you Happy now?!

      Denny kicks the dash
      Hard
      A loud Crack

      Pause

KY. Denny

      Denny pouts

KY. Hey

      Denny pouts

KY. okay
      you asked for it
      heeeere it comes
      heeeere comes the Horse Face

      he makes the Horse Face

KY. neeeeigh
      Hello Denny
      remember me?
      I'm Carla
      You took me to Homecoming last year

DENNY. stop

KY. While you were Dancing with all the Pretty Girls
      I was outside grazing on the Football Field
      neeeeeeeeeeeiiiiiiiiiiiggggggghhhh

DENNY. Stop!

      Ky stops

he laughs
he squeezes Denny's shoulder

KY. come on, Squirt
your Dad's just having a little fun
I mean
that Carla was not an Attractive Girl

DENNY. yeah well I'm sure she's Way Prettier than your
Adulteress

Pause

KY. Denny –

The Car Slows

KY. Oh for Christ's Sake

Ky smacks the Steering Wheel

KY. Yeah
My Fuckin Tax Dollars at Work
Great

They better be adding a CARPOOL LANE

Ky cranes his neck Back and Forth

KY. We never should've stopped at In-N-Out

Ky cranes his neck Back and Forth

KY. What?
No one in this Lane has somewhere to Be?
Jesus Mother Loving Christ

Ky cranes his neck Back and Forth

DENNY. It's just Traffic

KY. well we have very important Dinner Plans

Ky cranes his neck Back and Forth

KY. Hey
Come on Pal
I'm trying to Get Over

Ky raises his hand Ironically

KY. Look at these Morons!

Yeah, I'm talking about you, Twat!

Since when is Construction a Free Pass for everyone to drive like Mr. fuckin Miyagi?!

Hey!

Come on!

We have DINNER PLANS!

He seethes
Ky grips the wheel
He gives up

DENNY. can we listen to My Music?

Please

Come On

I asked this time like You Said

Ky glances at Denny
He concedes

KY. Sure

Denny breathes a sigh of relief

DENNY. Finally

Denny rummages in his bag
He pulls out an iPod with an attached iTrip

He ejects Ky's CD

KY. Hey

gimme that CD

DENNY. Why?

Denny plays a quick game of keep away with his Dad
then puts the CD on the Dashboard

KY. Denny

come on

give it to me

Denny Ignores his Father
and finds a Play List He Likes

Denny's Music Plays

Something Bumpin
Gritty
Maybe a Little Too Dirty

DENNY. this is the Sound of the Streets

Denny grooves

DENNY. You like it?

Ky cranes his neck back and forth
He's too stressed about the Traffic to Care

KY. What?
Yeah Sure
Very Enthusiastic

DENNY. It's Pretty Tight, yeah?
oh this is the Best Part right here

Denny grooves to The Best Part

DENNY. You know who Really Loves this song?
Chris Ying
He plays it All the Time

KY. Okay Lady
I have my Blinker On –

Ky cranes his neck back and forth

KY. Who's Chris Ying?

DENNY. uh
Chris is at the House like All the Time

KY. Oh yeah?
then How come I never see Him?

DENNY. I don't know
cuz he comes over Right After School before you get
home from Work

Ky raises his hand Ironically

KY. Thank You!

DENNY. you know

You could meet him if you came home from work Early
sometimes like Mom asks —

KY. well How come he never stays for Dinner?

I'm paying the Mexicans to build a Porch for a Reason,
you know

and your Mom's got that new Caesar recipe she's been
waiting to Try Out

Ask him to stay sometime, Squirt

We can show him what a couple of genuine Grillmeisters can Do, Huh?

Ky nudges Denny

KY. Wockawockawockawockawockawockawockawock-
awockawockawocka

He cranes his neck back and forth

KY. oh Now what's this Asshole doing?

DENNY. His Dad's got him playing for like a Billion Soccer
Teams so he's Always got Practice

KY. This is your Coach's Son?

DENNY. Duh

KY. I thought you didn't like that Kid

DENNY. yeah he's kinda Lame

but this way I can get in Good with Coach Ying —

Ky throws up his hands

KY. oh come on Jerk Off

DENNY. like Last Week when Coach Ying was leaving the
House

I told him how I really want to play Sweeper even
though most Coaches don't let you play Sweeper until
you're at least Eleven and Coach Ying told me he'd
totally Let Me Try

Denny grooves

KY. What do you mean Leaving the House
when he picked up Chris?

DENNY. no

> Coach Ying comes over to the House too

KY. oh yeah?

> You guys play in the backyard together or what?

DENNY. Nah

> All Chris ever wants to do is play Playstation in My Room

KY. then What's your Coach Do?

> *Denny shrugs*

DENNY. He swims in the Pool mostly

KY. He Swims

> in our Pool?

DENNY. Yeah

> well sometimes he eats first
>
> which is Weird
>
> cuz you're not supposed to swim after you eat, Right?

KY. well he must like to Swim

DENNY. I guess

> *Denny Grooves*

DENNY. You know

> Chris has the New Crash Bandicoot

> *Ky cranes his neck back and forth*

KY. so

> What's your Coach do after he swims?

DENNY. uh

> Sometimes he comes upstairs and says Hi to me and Chris

KY. Oh yeah?

DENNY. Uh huh

> He asks How We're doing

KY. Then what?

DENNY. Then

> I don't know

He Usually tells Chris they're gonna Go Soon

KY. Yeah?

and they Go?

Ky cranes his neck back and forth

DENNY. Not Right Away

First he tells Chris he'll be Downstairs

and to come get him when we're finished with our game

then he asks me if it's okay if he closes my Door

KY. What do you say?

DENNY. Sure

I don't care if my Door's closed or not

Ky cranes his neck back and forth

KY. Finally

The Car picks up Speed

Denny grooves
He watches the landscape zoom by

DENNY. Whoa

Maywood

Mom says Maywood's where all the Gang Bangers Live

Like there's this Big Guy in Fifth Grade who's from Maywood

And whenever you ask him about Maywood he always shouts like on MTV like

"May*wood*!: Up To No *Good*!"

Do you think he's a Gang Banger?

KY. I don't know, Squirt

DENNY. I don't think Coach Ying goes Downstairs

Ky turns Denny's Music down

DENNY. Why'd you do that?

KY. What do you mean You don't think he goes Downstairs?

DENNY. Dad –

KY. Why don't you think he goes Downstairs?

Denny shrugs

DENNY. cuz I hear things sometimes

KY. Like what?

DENNY. I don't Know
   like Things
   Like through my Door
   Across the Hall
   I can hear Something

KY. Something Loud?

DENNY. no

KY. So Quiet?

DENNY. mm Kinda Loud and Quiet I guess
   Like when I hear it
   I make Chris press Pause
   then we put our Ears to the door
   and we can hear it every time
   and it sounds like
   Like
   I guess
   Like Shaking

KY. Then what?

DENNY. Then Chris and Coach Ying Go Home

Denny turns the music back up
He grooves
Ky turns it back down

DENNY. Dad –

KY. What about your Mom?
   What's she do?

DENNY. She doesn't really do anything

KY. No?

DENNY. Uh uh
   After they Leave

    she Just sits in front of the TV
    in her Hard Rock Cafe shirt

KY. her Hard Rock Cafe shirt

DENNY. yeah
    you know
    the Really Big One
    the one that's so Big she doesn't need to wear pants

    Ky drives
    and Drives
    And Drives

    The Car Moves Way Too Fast

DENNY. Hey Dad
    Slow Down
    Where are you going?
    Dad?
    What's Wrong, Dad?
    I'm Scared

KY. your Dad
    your Dad's just –

DENNY. Dad
    I wanna go Home
    do we get to go home soon?

KY. Denny – !
    look
    you just
    you gotta Trust Me, okay?

DENNY. Is there Trouble?

KY. hey hey
    there's No Trouble

DENNY. I wanna Call Mom

KY. No!
    no
    there's no need to Involve your Mother

and the Car starts to Shake
Louder and Louder

and through the Windows
we can see Pine Trees flying past the car

DENNY. Dad?

    BOY. the Lord is Good

DENNY. You said it wasn't Real

    BOY. a Stronghold in the Day of Trouble

DENNY. Where are you going?

    BOY. and he knows those who Trust in Him

the Shaking Stops
the Pine Trees are Gone
and Ky spies the CD on the Dashboard

KY. Hey

    gimme that CD

DENNY. Why?

KY. Denny

    come on

    give it to me

Denny rolls his eyes
He grabs the CD
and plays a quick game of keep away with his Dad

but before handing it to his father
he catches a Glimpse of the Label
the CD is suddenly a Strange Shade of Maroon
Denny freezes
<u>He looks at the CD for a long time</u>

KY. Squirt?

    come on

    it's gonna get Scratched

    Denny –

DENNY. Is she gonna be at the apartment?

KY. Who?

Denny holds up the CD

DENNY. Darcy the Starbucks Barista
Is she gonna be there when we get there?

Ky glances over
BUSTED

KY. okay
first of all, Squirt
she's a Musician

DENNY. Oh Cool
She gonna sing us some of her shitty Christian Chick
Rock?

Denny throws the CD to his feet

KY. look, Denny
Darcy
She's a Good woman
a Woman of God

DENNY. so she Is gonna be there

Pause

KY. She's uh
She's really thrilled to meet you

Ky smiles

KY. We're gonna Grill tonight
Just the Three of us
We just got this little grill for our Deck
The Deck's not so big but it's got a Nice View of the
Neighborhood

Darcy's an Amazing Cook
Really
You won't believe It

I told her how much you like Caesar Salad
so she's breaking out her Special Caesar recipe
I mean

I've had a lot of Caesars, Squirt
but Darcy's?
Wooo

How's that for a Surprise?
Huh?
the Grillmeisters Back in Action!
see
Aren't you Glad you didn't Spoil your appetite?
Plenty of room for Steak

"The Juice, Dad"
"The Juice"

Ky tousles Denny's hair

KY. Wockawockawockawockawockawockawockawock-
awockawockawockawocka

Denny smacks his Father's Hand away

DENNY. Don't touch me

KY. you know
I knew about your Mom and that Man for Years!
but did I say anything?
No!

Denny looks at his Father in disbelief

KY. that's right
cuz I thought that Maybe
Maybe –
but Of Course
as soon as I make One Mistake
I'm the Bad Guy

god

Denny pouts
Ky softens

KY. hey

Denny pouts

KY. denny

Denny mutters

DENNY. church freak faggot

> *Ky pinches Denny*
> *Way Too Hard*

DENNY. ow!

ow!

> *Ky tries to Hold it Together but Can't*

KY. How do you think you got on that Spring All-Stars Team in the First Place, Huh?

you think it's just a Coincidence that your Coach didn't give you the time of day until he started Nailing your Mom?

Huh?

Oh No

I'm Sorry

I forgot

It's because you're such a Great Sweeper, Right Denny?

> *the Windows turn a Strange Shade of Maroon*
> *and the Squiggles and Static of a Child's Imagination*
> *become the Squiggles and Static of a Child's Nightmare*

KY. and Guess what?

not only did your Mother Fuck your Way onto That Team

but Every Team you ever played for

If your Mom weren't so Quick to Give It Away

you never would've made Club

or Varsity

or Any of It

Simple as That!

> *Denny curls up*

KY. I don't know why she gave you the idea you could Play Soccer to begin with

I mean

let's be Honest, Denny
with your Abilities
the best you can hope for is Maybe
Maybe
if you're Lucky
Coaching a bunch of Ten year-olds on the Weekends

Denny starts Crying
a faint voice through the Speaker

> **BOY.** Coach Denny –

KY. Hey
Someone had to tell you Sooner or Later

> **BOY.** Coach Denny –

KY. and it's Better that it comes from Someone who Loves
you

> **BOY.** Coach Denny –

Something in the World Shakes Loose

KY. come on
Cut It Out
Wocka
It's all a Scam anyway
Wockawocka
I tell you, Squirt
You think you know what it takes to Love someone and
Wockawockawocka
I'm gonna let you in on a little Secret:
You see these two fingers here
What you want to do is slip these inside Her Nice and
Gentle
then Wocka Wocka back and forth like this
Slow at first then Faster
you Got it?
now Meanwhile
You wanna crook your thumb back like this
Yeah?

and you wanna press that right up against her Clit
Not too hard
Not too soft
You guys win?
Wockawocka
Is that a Yes or a No?

the Squiggles become more Abstract more Terrifying
the Feelings you keep tucked away in the deepest parts of your
Mind and Body

KY. I told Darcy how much you loved her Caesar Salad,
Squirt
Wocka
and pretty soon
She'll Cum Her Brains Out
I swear to God
and from there, Squirt
Wockawockawocka
She's All Yours
I mean it
She'll do Whatever The Fuck You Want
You guys win?
I mean I've had a lot of Caesars in my Lifetime, Wocka
but Darcy's?
Wooo

it Suddenly becomes Very Dark
Denny turns to the Audience and Speaks at 85 Miles Per
Hour

DENNY. She makes the dressing from Scratch
A full clove of Garlic
Six Egg whites
Two Cans of Anchovies
and a half pound of Parmesan
She marinates the Lettuce in Lemon Juice for Two
Hours

and when it's time to toss the salad
Instead of Tongs
she uses her Hands
She paints her fingernails Maroon
The Polish makes her Hands look like Fungus

a Voice through the Speakers
it's on a Loop

    BOY. Coach –

DENNY. She doesn't Toss the salad so much as she Rubs it
She Rubs It Hard
Like So Hard the muscles in her hands and triceps Twitch
and Sweat begins to Drip Down from her Armpits
and Pretty Soon
the Lettuce
the Dressing
the Parmesan

    BOY. Coach –

DENNY. It all turns Maroon
and the Maroon
It Bleeds Upwards
From her Fingers to her Shoulders
and Before I know It
Both Her Arms are Deep Maroon
and she sweats Thick Caesar Dressing down her Body
and the Caesar smell mixes with her Perfume
and the Smell crawls out of the Kitchen and into my Nostrils
and Shakes my Brain Loose it's So So Strong

    BOY. Coach –

DENNY. then you come up from Behind Her, Dad
and she slips her Fingers into your Mouth
and you start to Suck Off the Dressing
you Suck So Hard
you Suck So Hard

that you Suck off her Skin

    BOY. Coach –

DENNY. then you Suck off her Muscles and her Veins and
her Tendons

    BOY. Coach –

DENNY. and you Suck Off her Organs last of All
till she's Nothing but Bone

    BOY. Coach –

DENNY. and now Sometimes, Dad
when I have Sex
I pretend that I'm You
and that the Girl's Darcy
and then I Do It to her Really Hard

    BOY. Coach –

DENNY. like she tells me it Hurts
but that just makes me do it Harder
and Harder
till she's Crying
and then when I'm Close

    BOY. Coach –

DENNY. I like Pull Out
Hold her Down with my Forearm
and put It Right Up Next to Her Face till she's Nothing
but Bone

Ky turns on the Headlights

*He is joined by the Headlights of Other Cars cruising along
the 5 at Dusk
there are Way Too Many to Count
and The World is Suddenly Much Larger than We Thought*

KY. what do you think of Her?
Pretty great huh?
your Dad's never gonna walk down That Aisle again
but Darcy
How would you feel if we got married?

Wockawockawockawockawockawockawocka
I'm Sorry, Son
but God commanded it
that was a Beautiful Ceremony
and you know what the most Special Part was?
Having you up there at the Altar
and that Passage you Read
Nahum 1:7
Wockawocka
How's your mom?

More and More Headlights
Brighter and Brighter
Faster and Faster
the World Begins to Peel Apart

DENNY. Dad
When do I get to Go Home, Dad?
Dad
I wanna Go Home, Dad
When do I get to Go Home?
Dad

KY. Times are Tough, Squirt
Work Work Work Work
Fred
Fred let me Go
You're the Reason I Work Up in the Morning
you believe that?
All those Weekends I spent at a Shredder like a Wocka-
wocka instead of at your Games
and for Work?
Sun and Moon and Work
None of it's Real
Work Work Work Work Work

DENNY. You get off your ass and find a Job yet?

Ky shrugs

DENNY. Is that a Yes or a No?

KY. How's your Mom?
   She gonna be at your Graduation?

   Denny shrugs

KY. And what about what's-his-name?

   Denny shrugs

KY. Don't tell your Mom but
   here's a little something for your Wockawocka
   Don't tell your Mom
   but lemme tell you, Squirt
   when your Dad was in College
   Wooo!
   how's Class?

DENNY. it's Okay

   Ky adjusts the rearview
   and the sound of Meat on a Grill
   sizzles through the Car Speakers for a Moment

KY. how come you Never Call?
   Gimme a Call
   why don't you Call?
   well Look Who Called

DENNY. Dad
   Don't tell Mom but
   We tried to be careful but

KY. You talk to your Mom?

   Denny shrugs

KY. She gonna be at your Graduation?
   Don't tell your Mom but
   she's gonna be at your Graduation

DENNY. Dad

KY. lemme guess: you need Money
   Is it about Money?
   You gotta be more Responsible with your Money

DENNY. I hope you realize who I'm adopting this attitude
  problem from

  the sound of Children Chasing a Soccer Ball
  whooshes through the Car Speakers

KY. don't tell your Mom
  but out of the Blue
  Darcy
  she just packed it up
  Out of the Blue

DENNY. Dad
  when do I get to go Home, Dad?

KY. Out of the Blue

DENNY. You think you know what it takes to Love Someone

KY. She just packed it up

DENNY. Seriously, Dad
  One Day you're gonna

  the sound of a Speeding Rollercoaster

KY. how's Work?

DENNY. it's Good
  you know I think Ted's gonna give me that Raise

KY. what do you think of her?
  Pretty Great, huh?

DENNY. that's Cool

KY. yeah it is but
  out of the Blue
  Jessica
  she just packed it up

DENNY. Dad
  when do I?

KY. Out of the Blue
  Maggie
  she just

  the Sound of Air-Conditioned Lovers

DENNY. you know what Ted had me do today?
> Can you believe that?
> A man my

KY. how's your new place?

> *Denny shrugs*

KY. You seeing anyone?

> *Denny shrugs*

KY. well she sounds Great

> *Denny shrugs*

KY. hey Don't get Down on yourself, Squirt
> you're a Man –

DENNY. The Lord is Good

KY. and the truth is it's very difficult for a Man to Remain
> Faithful –

DENNY. a Stronghold in the Day of Trouble

KY. even to someone he Loves Very Much –

DENNY. and He knows those who
> Dad

> *the sound of a Body Gliding through a Pool*

KY. I know you're Coaching on the Weekends now
> but What do you mean you don't want Kids?

DENNY. Dad
> Where am I going, Dad?
> you know who I'm starting to look like, Dad?

> *the Sounds Overcome the Car*

KY. well that's what it's like

DENNY. Dad

KY. that's what it's like

DENNY. Dad

KY. that's what it's

DENNY. Dad

> *a Hush of Moonlight flickers through the rearview
> as the Car leaves the Road*

to float above the Sun and Moon and Stars

Ky speaks softly
Tenderly
like we've never heard him before

KY. I knew
    I swear to God
    Don't Ask me How
    but from the moment she told me
    I knew
    a Son
    I was gonna have a Son
    was I Scared

    but I knew   **DENNY.**
    I knew from the   hey
    moment she told me   I remember
    I knew   you'd pick me up after
    a Son   my Games
    I was gonna have a Son   and I mean I'm little
    was I Scared   little
    but I knew   you'd pick me up after
                                            my Games
                                            I remember
                                            you'd pick me up, Dad
                                            you remember that?

KY. oh I remember
DENNY. you'd pick me up
KY. I'd pick you up
DENNY. and you'd say
    you'd Say
    you'd Say

    A Sudden Silence
    A Long Quiet

    Ky adjusts the Rearview

KY. You guys win?

    and Suddenly we're back on the 5

on a Saturday Afternoon with the Sun so Bright
the Windows are Windows
and Denny shrugs like a Down and Dirty Kid

KY. I mean it, Squirt
Honest to God
the Sun and Moon and Stars

Voices through the Speakers:

> **BOY.** Coach Denny –
> **MAN.** yeah Squirt?
> **BOY.** how close are we to Silver Lake?
> **MAN.** Pretty Close
> **BOY.** how close?

the Voices become a Soft Hiss

DENNY. Dad –

KY. Yeah Squirt?

DENNY. How close are we?

KY. Pretty close

DENNY. I'm Scared

KY. hey there's no need to be Scared, Pal
we're in this Together

and the Windows are full of Static
but the Static
very slowly
begins to Transform

DENNY. but are we gonna be there Soon?

KY. well once this Traffic lets up

DENNY. but there isn't any Traffic

KY. Of course there's Traffic
Look at all the Cars

Denny wipes at the Windows

DENNY. Those are Trees, Dad
They're Trees
Dad

    Where are we, Dad?

KY. it's a Surprise

DENNY. what kind of Surprise?

KY. We're on the Matterhorn, Squirt

    and the Static is Snowfall

DENNY. the Matterhorn?

    but we passed Disneyland

    whoa

    it's Snowing, Dad

KY. See?

    your Dad's not a Bad Guy after all

DENNY. You said the Matterhorn Wasn't a Real Mountain –

KY. The Lord is good –

DENNY. but it's really Snowing –

KY. a Stronghold in the Day of Trouble

DENNY. Dad

KY. Work Work Work WorkWorkworkworkworkworkwork –

DENNY. It's Really Snowing, Dad!

    Look Dad

    the Snow, Dad

    the Snow!

It begins to Snow from the Ceiling of the Theater
The Snow falls from Everywhere
It's <u>Amazing</u>
<u>Breathtaking</u>
but while the Snow falling past the Windows seems Real
the Snow falling from the Ceiling is made of Shredded Paper
Scraps
Hole punches:
the Lost Time of a Man Who Works Weekends
Work Work Work Work Work
It Doesn't Stop

the Stage Fills with It

and Voices come through the Speakers again
Denny and a Boy's
but this time
Ky and Denny seem to gesture
in relation to the voices on the radio
Ky gestures with Denny's voice while Denny
gestures with the Boy's

    BOY. Is that the field?

    DENNY. yep

Denny looks out the Window
He watches the Landscape Slow Down

the Car is Still
lots of Sunlight

    BOY. Where's the rest of the team?

    DENNY. I guess we beat em

Ky cranes his neck back and forth

    DENNY. Wow

        crowded on the Weekends huh?

        tell me if you see a Spot

    BOY. There!

    DENNY. where?

    BOY. right there!

    DENNY. oh

        Good

        Eyes

Ky starts to Park
He backs into the Spot

    BOY. Coach Denny –

    DENNY. Yeah Squirt?

    BOY. You think I could play Forward today?

    DENNY. Forward?

    BOY. yeah

    DENNY. but you're our Best Sweeper

BOY. I know
  but I've never scored a Goal before

The Car comes to a Stop

DENNY. okay
  I tell you what
  you can play Forward at the top of the Second
  Half
  how's that?

BOY. thanks Coach Denny!

DENNY. on Two Conditions –

BOY. Conditions?

DENNY. Uh huh
  first:

  you run some Offensive Drills with me before
  the game

BOY. okay

DENNY. and Second:

  you let me ask your Mom out

BOY. you really wanna ask my Mom out?

Ky nods

BOY. do you think you can make her Happy?

DENNY. well

  I think I can try

They Unbuckle their Seat Belts

Ky reaches into the backseat
He pulls away the Coat

a Nylon Bag full of Soccer Gear is Underneath

Ky steps Out of the Car with the Bag of Soccer Gear

Ky stands in the Snow
as he sets up Two Red Cones that represent a Goal

the Field goes on as Far as the Eye Can See

Denny gets out of the Car
and runs in the Snow towards Ky

Ky tosses a Soccer Ball to Denny
the Ball stops at Denny's feet

Denny maneuvers through the Snow with the Ball
His Cleats and Ball leave Tracks

Denny kicks the Ball at Ky
Ky makes a Great Save

He grips the Ball tight
and gives it a good Hard overhead Throw

Denny chases after the Ball
as Ky watches him Run
Like he's the Only Thing that Matters in the World

and very Far Away
we might just see
a Man dressed like He Works Weekends
watching the two of them Play Together in the Snow

End

A Note About "Time Shifts"

While working in collaboration with Anne Kauffman, Page 73 Productions, Soho Rep, two marvelous actors, and a crack team of designers, I
discovered that theatrical "time shifts" throughout Sixty Miles to Silver
Lake are an extremely helpful tool in shaping a full production. I'm
wary of being too prescriptive about the nature of these "shifts," how
subtle or conspicuous, or how frequently they ought to occur – only that
it's my feeling that, well, they really ought to occur.

The trick is to maintain the fluidity of a single sixty mile car ride while
simultaneously delineating stark changes in attitude, temperature, and
age over many, many years. Therefore these "shifts" ought to be deliber-
ate but restrained; inventive and resourceful.

– D.L.